OUR BROTHER HAS DOWN'S SYNDROME

AN INTRODUCTION FOR CHILDREN

Written by
Shelley Cairo, Jasmine Cairo and Tara Cairo

Photographs by
Irene McNeil

Designed by
Helmut W. Weyerstrahs

Annick Press Ltd.
Toronto • New York

Design and graphic realization by Helmut W. Weyerstrahs.
Custom colour enlargements by Japan Camera Centre 1 Hour Photo

Sixth printing, April 1995

Annick Press Ltd.

Annick Press gratefully acknowledges the support of the
Canada Council and the Ontario Arts Council.

Canadian Cataloguing in Publication Data
Cairo, Shelley.
Our brother has down's syndrome

ISBN 0-920303-30-7 (bound). – ISBN 0-920303-31-5 (pbk.)

1. Down's syndrome – Juvenile literature.
2. Mentally handicapped children – Family relationships –
Juvenile literature. I. Cairo, Jasmine.
II. Cairo, Tara. III. McNeil, Irene. IV. Title.

RJ506.D68C34 1985   j649'.152   C85-098788-1

Distributed in Canada by:
Firefly Books Ltd.
250 Sparks Avenue
Willowdale, ON
M2H 2S4

Published in the U.S.A. by Annick Press (U.S.) Ltd.
Distributed in the U.S.A. by:
Firefly Books (U.S.) Inc.
P.O. Box 1338
Ellicott Station
Buffalo, NY 14205

 Printed on acid-free paper.

Printed and bound in Canada by
D.W. Friesen & Sons, Altona, Manitoba

Hello.
Our names are Tara and Jasmine and we would like to tell you about our little brother, Jai.

There is something special about Jai. He has Down's Syndrome. Maybe you have a brother or sister who has Down's Syndrome, or have a friend who does.

We want to tell you what it is like for us and Jai.

Mostly Jai is like every other brother or sister in the world. Sometimes he's fun and sometimes he's not, but no matter what, we love him very much.

Maybe you would like to know what Down's Syndrome is. Did you know that your body is made up of cells? In kids our size there are trillions of cells. They are so small that you can only see them with a microscope. Inside the cells there are even tinier things called chromosomes. Most people have 46 chromosomes in each of their cells: 23 from their mother and 23 from their father. Jai, like other people with Down's Syndrome, has 47 chromosomes in each of his cells, all so tiny that we can't even see them. The number of Jai's chromosomes was decided inside Mom's body even before we knew that she was going to have a baby.

Here is a drawing of a cell :

Here is a drawing of a chromosome :

It takes people with Down's Syndrome a longer time to learn to do things. They also look a bit different from other people, but mostly they look like their families.

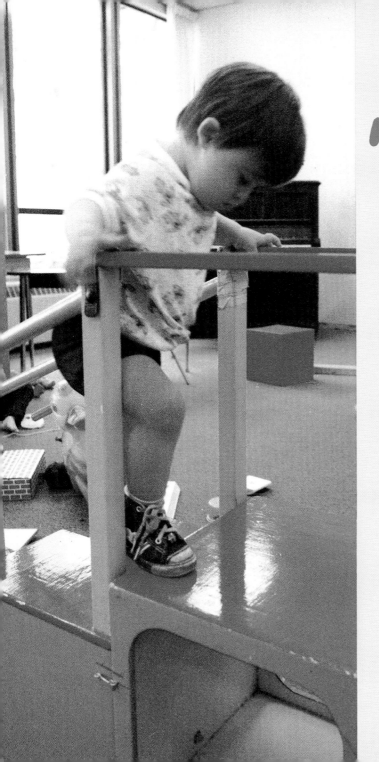

There isn't a way to make Down's Syndrome go away but there are many things we can do to help people with Down's Syndrome. We help Jai mostly by playing with him and talking to him a lot and giving him lots of love.

Two times a week Jai goes to a special play group where he practises all the things he is learning to do, like climbing stairs…

...eating with a spoon, doing things with his hands and playing with the other kids.
When Jai is older he will go to Kindergarten at our school.

Now and then Diane, who is Jai's teacher, comes to our home to talk with our mom about how Jai is doing. She helps us find good ways to help Jai learn to do things like build with blocks and things like that.

Although we help Jai in special ways, mostly we do things with him as anyone does with their brother or sister…

…like reading stories…

…and walking on the beach.

Jai can be such a trouble maker sometimes.

You should see him
when he gets into our stuff.

Mom and Dad have to give him more
attention because he's little. That's the way
it is with little brothers and sisters.

It makes us sad when we hear other kids and grown-ups call people names like "retarded" or make fun of handicapped people.
We know now that anyone could have a brother or sister who is handicapped. Handicapped people are just as special as everyone else.

Jai may not talk as much as other kids his age, and it took him longer to learn to walk. We spend more time teaching him things but he cries like other kids and he smiles like other kids.

He is curious about the world…

…just like other kids.

He likes animals...

...and he likes to play
monster with our dad.

He likes Santa
and loves going
for a swing…

...and loves ice cream!...

...and he gives terrific kisses!

Jai may be a little different (we *all*
have different things about us),
but mostly he's just like the rest of us.